Memories and Insights

MAYANK MOHAN PANDE

ISBN 979-8-88849-096-9

Contents

The Rogue of Guliapani

This is a story of an elephant who became a rogue,

And I, a young lad of 14, as was then in vogue,

accompanied my father the local Forest Brass,

On a forest inspection, and noticed on the grass,

On that day of 19 Jan 1970, the footprint of a JUMBO,

With dew all around it, and none in the hollow.

Do you realize dear reader, why this is a clear sign,

Of an elephant's presence at that point of time?

We were in a jeep with passengers one less than nine,

And ahead of us was a fire line,

Which as you know, is a clearing between two woods,

That prevents one from burning if the other should,

Across the fire line, lay a freshly uprooted tree,

When one of the passengers yelled a sound eerie,

"HATHI" he shouted, and we all looked ahead,

Our hearts pierced with fear and dread,

A jolt shook us, and numbed my mind,

Before it was realised, we had been struck from behind,

The driver "Giri" in a flash of divine inspiration,

Thought once of jumping out,

but bravely reverted back to his obligation,

And drove right into the river a few miles ahead.

Through a poacher's track which we just then found,

Into the security of "Banbasa" army camp,

Which from that place, Guliapani was ten miles around.

The Lord spared us so that I may write this story,

And ponder why men or mammoths make lives sorry,

Is it the degradation of those who were once held in esteem,

That make rogues behave the way they do, and let off
steam?

Sheljam

Down the memory lane, there is a forest rest house in the woods.

Colonial in style, it is of a vintage where a large hand-pulled punkah, delivered the goods.

The furniture was still fine, with a good old gun-rack.

How I wish those days could come back.

A sloping roof, a stable converted in to a garage.

An Awla tree in the surrounding acreage.

Out-houses in a row, an outdoor kitchen.

It also had a wood-fired hot-case,

with the suggestion of game and chicken.

Under the bright light of the Petromax we read Edgar Allan Poe,

Perry Mason and James Hadley Chase.

This fond memory no nightmare can erase.

No newer dreams and ecstasies can these ones fully displace.

'Murgee'

The wild fowl is known as the 'jungli murgee',

The food of jackals, cats and yours truly.

A shotgun is needed if you don't have a two-two,

Now that shooting is banned, there is not much to do.

Except go to the market and see a less sporting slaughter,

Without fun of the chase and a rare encounter.

A jungli murgee was more difficult to get, than a broiler chicken can be,

More often he beat you, and that's why he is called the jungli murgee.

Of our murgee again there are two kinds,

One with a shiny black plumage, a name called 'Kaliz',

which only in the mountains a hunter finds.

The other is orange and equal in taste.

I could never shoot a murgee because I was always in haste.

This Hissing Silence

Over the meadows, in the mountain tops,

The wind blows, hisses, and never stops.

The same kind of silence, in this office room I find,

Of other abilities left far behind.

I sit here and compose,

Of prickly thorns, and a lovely rose.

Have you seen an 'Awla' tree?

The fruit Is the purest form of Vitamin C,

And under which the deer roam free.

If you have, you'll feel the hiss,

Otherwise, there's not much amiss,

Because this hissing silence will always be.

Confusion

After many years I heard the pitter-patter of the rain,

And I began to collect my wits which remain.

To sympathetic ears narrate,

This pain and this confused mental state.

When the mind is full of all that has to be done,

And bewilderment inhibits the commencement of any one,

Remote from the state of bliss, this is some kind of paralysis.

Let us not brood over this malady,

And work out a remedy.

If I just give my work some prioritization,

God will restore my concentration.

The Little Fawn

From the stillness of the dawn,

Emerged this little fawn.

Right below the Awla tree.

Feeling alive and feeling free.

Feeling that nature was kind.

Alas a hunter pulled the trigger,

And the little fawn, left the world behind.

Tears for My Rajah

There are times when men resort to arms in acts of retribution,

At others they leave such matters to the Lord and

beat their chests in compunction for their own sins,

but whenever a valiant soul departs, adversary or mate, they all weep.

These then are my tears for Rajah.

"Dear Rajah, as you depart to the heavenly sky,

Your loved ones look above, with a tearing wail and a helpless cry,

'O' a better friend to us than human beings can be,

May you find your heavenly abode, as a tranquil sea.

Life and partners, are a transient gift of the Lord,

but we will always be in a state of pain.

The sighful memories of your love,

beauty and friendship will forever remain."

Spring

The earth came closer to the sun,

Cheerful birds began to sing.

The 'Bihu' dancers joyfully proclaimed the arrival of Spring.

The climate warmed and the spirits began to rise:

All remembered this saying of the wise:

That in this world miseries, and joys, abound.

Is it merely because the orbit of the earth is not perfectly round?

No, because happiness is possible in all kinds of weather.

We must just love and be loved together.

Quake

The earth trembled, shaking all around

Brought to an end the Journey to where all are bound.

Though the marks you get in college matter in life,

They are those that matter most which you leave behind, with the help of your wife.

Reflecting on what before God is more Important,

One realizes that it is better to be humble than insolent.

Love

Love is between two beings or between one and many,

Love is a gift of the Lord, to help us resolve conflicts and live in harmony.

That this is not always possible is a very hard fact,

Jesus and Krishna revealed that despite anything we must surrender,

And just for the day our roles positively enact.

Love is a caress, a gentle kiss, a hand to hold,

A step towards fulfilment despite heat and cold.

We are midway in being men and

Love helps us to endure, many times ignore and when required to be bold.

Love is not to give alms but to kindle hope and pass on

Ability to the less fortunately placed,

It is protecting the weak from the slashes of malice, sword and gun.

Love is to send to thugs a message to mend their ways
before we love them,

We'll not permit this kind of fun.

Love is what Jesus practiced, as did Lord Rama, the
Prophet, Buddha, Mahavir, Guru Nanak and Gandhi,

All lovers of the Creator.

The same cruelties were even then present,

Without stealing their bliss and an internal gentle laughter.

These great men positively smiled at life and at our Maker,

Without lightning, sans thunder, just a gently purring
electric motor.

Love is between man and woman in the full moon's light.

With a salute to the sunset, wishing the World a good night.

Law

For most of my life I saw,

A gross deviation from the laid down law.

This violation was within and without,

With actions resulting from the world of doubt.

One good thing about this feature,

Is that in this universe there are disciplining forces of nature.

Let me be whipped, the rascals hanged.

There is something wrong with the law of the land.

Engineering

There was a man called Gibbs, not Gibbings,

Who removed us of our misgivings,

That not only, in heating, we must put in work,

But that also in cooling, we can't from this requirement shirk.

There was a man called Sylvanus P. Thompson,

Who presented the Calculus as a gramme and not a tonne,

His book was called 'Calculus Made Easy',

Which made many a Math Prof uneasy,

By his statement that "What one fool can do, another could!",

Which meant those that are haughty stand on high stools of wood,

Which can be lowered or accessed easily even while munching biscuits,

Let us salute Sylvanus P. Thompson, who incidentally invented 3-phase circuits!

Cowdung Embers

Through 14 chilly Himalayan nights, warmed by wood
fired by cowdung embers,
A loving son, his departed father, fondly and with sorrow
remembers.

A scholar, a saint and mentor to him was he, to the end his
mathematics strong.
Despite what others did to him he could do no one any wrong.

A student of the great physicist Krishnan at Allahabad was
he and became a forester by trade,
Reared in penury, he did not do much to let that weakening
spirit fade.

For him some sloth, fear and resignation was a more
comfortable life,
From a well to do doctor's progeny, was my good mother,
an educated lady not adept at housekeeping,
his for 50 years a very good wife.

Misery and pain I want to forget and forgive,

I want to offer all offenders an olive.
This is so because most of our life was so grand,
Full of learning, a regal childhood and through our
teachers and parents all of us brothers and sister on our feet
comfortably and proudly stand.

Memories thus I pull out, of colonial hearths and mantles,
Of sloping roofs, outdoor kitchens, jungles,
mountains, servants, bungalows, jeeps, a 1949 Ford Deluxe,
of pebble strewn roads, wooden bridges, mahauts, streams
and fine old crockery fed with water boiled in wood fired
stoves & soot covered kettles.

This epitaph which I have today begun
will by the grace of the Lord one day in many chapters end.
If for nothing else my Baba's memory will all to knowledge
and goodness bend.

Sensuality

Let us talk of sunsets and not volcanos,

Of the warmth of a mountain hearth and not scorching infernos.

There are forms chiselled to perfection, garnished with smiles,

Leading to fantasies of a thousand miles.

Why does the Nilakanthan the poison not swallow?

In the company of Parvati in the glorious Himalayan nights?

An unbridled lust will lead to ugliness and dirty fights.

The warmth that forms give us let warmth alone be,

I will not let the scorch of this furnace come close to me.

The form, the smiles, the movements and the gait, will always combine some elements inside,

Let sunsets be beautiful sunsets, and us to our vows abide.

Dreamer

I am a dreamer and always have been,

Dreaming of things few have seen,

Of Science, Technology and the Laser beam,

Of sunsets and beauty,

A King and a Queen.

Paranoia

At times I sink into a quagmire of doubt,

Full of suspicion, tinges of fear and feelings inside that want
to make me shout.

WHY should I be belittled and not allowed to grow?

When God has given me of my subjects the know.

Falling thus into anger and despair,

Seeking loving ones for my soul's repair,

I end up calling up my wife Jaishri, telling her that the
world may do me harm.

"RELAX", she assures me as usual,"

It is PARANOIA: you have taken your medicines,

think of God,

there is no cause for alarm!"

Jettison

I was tempted every day, I swayed in every way,

But my morals always held their sway.

Now I shed behind all feelings of that kind,

To see whether I can really build an understanding of applied atomic structure,

At the same time trying to find,

An outlet for my creativity in engineering and literature.

Assisted by my daughter and son, associated with my caring wife,

The day has come for me to draw satisfaction from life.

My Tears for the Homeless

A job robbed, a family uprooted to freeze under the sky,

A frail mother, a small girl and a just older brother,

hit hard yet not being able to shriek, why?

The proud father not willing to live on dole,

goes far away for a job to find.

After some wait his helpless family feels he has left them all behind.

Thus, the first tear from my saddened eye did drop,

When much filthy lust on the poor mother did crop.

It is unjust to fight wars unless against poverty they be.

It is criminal to engage in the rotten game of- none better than we.

When our families suffering in penury come within our sight,

The least we can do is to pray,

That the Almighty strengthen them to put up an honourable fight.

And give a pie to every child that the windshield does shine,

Perchance his need and plight are full of fear and pain that
is very genuine.

When the father returned the little girl clung to her Pop,

I heaved a sigh of relief, and that was my second tear-drop.

Decadence

Nature proceeds to disorder as scientists will agree,

Societies rot, as the junta has a spree.

A carcass remains of all animals including the mighty cats,

As of those of elephants, birds including bats.

Literature turns to titillate from one that entertained and informed,

Morals die to an extent that all laws get deformed.

Thus, we see decadence in all that is around.

But then the Lord takes over and sets the trends right,

By helping men to reverse nature's will by putting effort and a fight.

A fridge cools and dissipates heat, which is a pain,

But then the compressor works and the food cools again.

The Lord descends whenever matters go astray,

The dead had left continuity in life before they went away.

There is no thing as decadence in any permanent way,

It is just the Lord playing his game of swinging back and away.

Shillong

Yesterday, we drove up to Shillong,

It was beautiful and I was filled with the Lord's song.

That good and evil clash, within and without,

And the good in the end, will evil rout.

Is this because we are midway in becoming men?

If not, what is God's purpose then?

Why are forces of creation, the forces of lust?

Why does the same create men and the same lives do bust?

What is Lord Shiva, and what do our stories tell?

What is Maa Kamakhsi and why do they drive men to hell?

It is clear that our faith I have not understood.

Because faith is to believe, and not to uncover any hood.

Isn't it strange that we are like a sophisticated gadget.

That can think, and its progeny beget.

What is thought?

The mystery never ends.

Surely there is more to our stories,

than is credited by some friends.

As Winter Recedes

As winter recedes and spring draws near,

We must enjoy and spread happiness in the present and not live in the past or the future.

Let us recall and relive only pleasant memories, switching off those which make it difficult to cope,

And always look forward to the future with optimism and hope.

Have You Ever Wondered Why?

Radio waves are made and how they fly,

Making possible myriad applications,

Ranging from the internet to radar or even microwave ovens.

The story is very old,

Of Maxwell, Faraday, Coulomb, Volta, Ampere, Oersted,
Ohm, Tesla, Franklin, other greats whose feats are all gold.

Volta invented the battery and produced the flow of charge
called electric current,

Oersted discovered soon after that this flow in a straight wire,

caused a circular magnetic field, in the perpendicular
plane, to be present.

Faraday discovered that a changing magnetic field through,
say, a coil produced a voltage that is a source of electric field.

Very important outcomes did this finding yield.

It was left to Maxwell to prove that a changing electric field
across a condenser

with a dielectric within, produced a displacement current,
which we will soon explain.

For now, we notice it produced a magnetic field: Oersted all over again.

Now a capacitor we do recall, consists of two parallel conducting plates separated by an insulator,

which when connected to a battery, a DC voltage generator,

stores charge on its plates, the quantity being proportional to the voltage applied.

This is like the common rubber balloon which can store a volume of air depending on the pressure pumped inside.

When an alternating voltage is applied to a capacitor,

we see the positive charge on the top plate and the negative in the bottom one to increase as the voltage becomes greater and decrease as the voltage becomes smaller.

This flow of positive charge from and to the two plates of the condenser is as a time varying electric current seen,

despite the fact no charge can flow inside the condenser, because its plates are separated by an insulator in between.

This then is what the displacement current is about,

All very clear without any doubt.

Thus, in a wire if an oscillating current does flow,

A circular, also time varying magnetic field we find to grow.

Now this will produce still further a perpendicular changing electric field as per Faradays law.

Which will lead to a displacement current giving rise to a changing magnetic field again and further beyond,

And a wave propagates ahead on and on.

The Promise of Tomorrow

We came into this world and will one day return,

Why should this be a cause for sorrow?

Whatever we pursue we shall attain,

That is the promise of tomorrow.

The Winter of 1967

It was our winter vacation of 1967.

My father was the D.F.O. of Haldwani Forest Division,

Not possessing a private firearm, he was the custodian of a departmental shotgun.

At Chorgalia forest rest house we were camping,

Woken up by the bark of the kakar every morning.

And the call of the wild fowl called Junglee Murgee,

Luring me to carry the shotgun and into the jungle make a calculated entry.

My father thought hard on what could interest me more than shikar,

To tame my wild streak and take me afar.

The subject of calculus came as the answer for his troubled son.

And out came the classic tutorial 'Calculus Made Easy' by Silvanus P. Thompson.

The author incidentally was inventor of three phase circuits,

And hundreds who learnt calculus from his book
themselves became big hits.

For old times sake I recently ordered one,

From the online store amazon.com

My Tears for the Fatherless

I weep for one of the sisters in white,

Full of love, care, service and a future that is bright,

She is a sweet twenty and draws strength from the Holy Quran,

Peace and protection that cannot be given by man.

We cried when she told me her tale,

Scalding tears fell and our faces went pale.

She is the only child of her mother,

The riots of 1996 snatched away her caring father.

All religions are good, then why to those of other faiths we do harm?

Where the need is for peace and simplicity,

We have messed up our lives by dragging religion into our conflicts which are full of complexity.

We pray to the Lord not to dismember our land,

Bring health, happiness and peace to all his children by brushing us with his magic wand.

Eskimo

Written around 2006

He flew in a basket to Ahmedabad from Kolkata to join our family in 1998,

A jet black Labrador, he became the darling of our family, certainly did Eskimo the great.

As a pup he suffered from dehydration and to our bed post came and did shudder,

My wife and I dripped into his tiny mouth, drops of water mixed with Electral powder.

All these eight years he has been a guard and friend, whose instincts are against the mildest anarchy,

Whenever I so much as raised my voice, he'd jump at me and remind me of my duty.

My duty as head of the family, to ensure that all were in peace,

All Eskimo wants is love, and to be taken out twice a day on a leash.

A Merry Christmas and a Happy New Year

Came Christmas we beckoned our near and dear,

For dinner to celebrate our joy and the coming new year.

May 'Love' be the theme for 2007,

With peace declared all over the earth making a place for the Lord as it is in heaven.

We pray that a man's love of his wife be not dull,

But be of a class Shah Jahan had for Mumtaj Mahal.

His creation of such grand beauty and splendour,

Will serve as a monument of a bond second to none in grandeur.

Soothing Sights

Two stark facts stared me in the face, singing doom for what I cherish,

One that ultimately, I might grow blind,

The other that one day I must perish,

This made me resolve that as long as I have my eyesight I will SEE, that as long as I am not dead, I will LIVE and be kind.

My daughter Bhavya was at home for a break,

She encouraged me in all ways and insisted that to Lonawala we should go for a drive.

She and my wife Jaishri got together and with Sanjiv Kapoor's recipe baked a plum cake,

May the Lord make us make the most of the moments in which we are truly alive.

What beautiful mountains are our Western Ghats,

Even the old Mumbai-Pune highway was a pleasure to follow,

Thick with foliage and lots of fresh air, the road exists in old maps and charts.

With the scenery interspersed with many an old bungalow.

The next time my daughter came home on leave,

We hired a taxi to go and enjoy the sight of the sea,

To the Gateway of India, Marine drive, Nariman Point and nature parks, gems that have passed through a historic selective sieve,

The cup of tea, we had at the bank of the ocean was the ultimate in tranquility.

The Little Nuns

Binita and Nirmala, the girls in blue are little nuns
committed to a life with Christ.

In their early years they joined the mission, to SERVE and
do what is right.

Beds they make, pray for all and heal with their cheerful
smiles,

They study English and other subjects and I pray to the
Lord to give them joy and to carry them over many miles.

Jesus is their inspiration, Jesus is their strength,

May the Lord give them perennial joy and may they spread
over the earth's breadth and length.

the state of California until he was twenty-one. Being that Maggie was in New Mexico, she offered to take him. So a cholo from California found himself in a small town in New Mexico.

Shorty, the high school cheerleader loved by all, was the one the cholo decided to fall in love with. Now the Cabreras, the family that had taken Maggie in when the rest of the Sandovals moved to California, had a daughter, Alice, who was Shorty's best friend starting in elementary school. So Shorty's best friend was Frank's cousin!

Frank pined over Shorty for several years, and he told Alice's mom, Erlinda, "I'm going to marry Shorty," and the entire family burst out laughing, "Yeah right!"

Ironically, my dad and Tom became best friends when my dad moved to Gallup, and as fate would have it, he married Shorty's best friend, Alice, Frank's cousin!

Grandma and Grandpa Sandoval were raised in Mexico, so they spoke mostly Spanish. My mom and dad did not teach us how to speak Spanish, so I never had a meaningful conversation with Grandpa and Grandma Sandoval.

Maggie Sandoval, the oldest sister, and Daniel Hausner were married and built their strong relationship upon faith in the Holy Trinity. They lived in Gallup and were regulars at all the parties and functions held! My mom has said, "Auntie Maggie is my mother-in-law because she's here and has helped me with so much!"

My dad moving to Gallup got his sister Alice thinking that she would come to finish high school in Gallup as well. She is five years younger than my dad, so he had moved to live in Albuquerque when she was ready to move in with Auntie Maggie. So Auntie Maggie and Uncle Danny cared for two of the youngest Sandovals and put them through high school.

Auntie Maggie and Uncle Danny went to Mass every weekend, and everyone in the house was required to attend. A great love for God was fostered in the family, and all grew in faith and love with the Holy Trinity.

Grandpa Sandoval died when I was around five years old, but Grandma lived until I was in undergrad. I know that my dad loved his mom a lot. After her funeral, when I was twenty years old, he never said, "I love you," to me again until the Christmas before he died when I was forty-two! I have come to understand that losing a parent is a life-altering moment and can change all the meaningful relationships a person has developed.

5

And the child grew and became strong; he was filled
with wisdom, and the grace of God was on him.

—Luke 2:40

My best friend since birth, Maria—pronounced
Mah-ree-a in English and Muh-dee-a in Spanish—
has been a constant in my life. As a nonspeaker of
Spanish, I started calling her Mud in high school and
have never stopped! We were born into our friend-
ship. Her mom is Alice, my dad's younger sister. She
is only four months older than me, and she is my soul
sister. To this day, we remain so connected that many
times we have sent each other simultaneous text
messages, her in New Mexico and me in the United
States Virgin Islands!

However, my first nonrelative friend I met
when we were three years old. Granted, I am only
five days older than her, so there is a possibility that
we first met at the hospital! Her grandparents owned
a restaurant in Gallup, and my mom, Nana, and I
went there to eat. I was sitting in a booth, and a little
blonde-haired bluster came and sat right by me. As

fate would have it, her mom married a guy, and they moved three houses down the street from my family.

We lived on the "wrong side" of town, where houses were less expensive. So from day 1 of kindergarten, we started a routine: I would stop by her house, and we would walk to school together. The walking turned into bus riding, which turned into shared car rides with me driving.

Her stepdad was a real jerk, and he would beat her mom. Almost every Sunday, as my family was getting ready to go to 9:00 a.m. Mass, there would be a knock at the door. B——— would be bloody, and she'd ask my dad to go and talk to R———. Hence, I have no patience for domestic violence and can find no reasonable excuse for why it happens!

A——— and I were so close that my brothers treated her like a sister, and she would get picked on just as much as I did. When we were in middle school, John was in high school. It was fun to miss the bus, run back to the house, and ask him to give us a ride.

He finally had enough and said, "If you dorks miss the bus again, just walk to school." We were kind of intimidated by John, so the next time we missed the bus, we just started walking. John saw us walking over the overpass, pulled over, and through gritted teeth said, "Get in!"

A——— was so much a part of my family that Nana and Pa took her to Disneyland with me a couple of times. My brothers reached an age where sports started monopolizing their time, leaving just me. Rather than take me alone, they brought along a friend for me.

Val I have known since first grade. We started out as enemies in Ms. Foster's class and became frenemies until the sixth grade when we went to middle school. The idea of being in a brand new school and learning the ins and outs of changing classes, carrying books, and running for student council brought Val and me to a new place in our friendship. We soon became thick as thieves, so much so that other girls our age started calling us the Big Green Monster. We kind of were, but we were in our formative years, still trying to figure out this thing called life! We started our friendship at seven years old, and now at fifty-two years old, we still text and call each other often! We've lived different lives, but at the end of the day, our friendship has always remained strong.

When my mom told Mud and Val about what happened in Idaho, they came to my parents' house, and everyone cried and prayed.

I had the same boyfriend from my junior year of high school to my senior year of college. I've never been one to place all my hopes in a man, but I have always had a boyfriend. My first boyfriend in kindergarten, Chucky, and I still remain friends! So hopes were not placed in a guy, but fun was shared! My dad's rules were very strict when it came to me and boys. The rule was that I could not receive a phone call from a boy, much less anything else!

When I started high school, my dad decided that I could start having boyfriends. Of course, I picked a kid who was a punk rocker, rarely showered, and loved the Sex Pistols. It was not a hot and heavy relationship because I am Catholic and adhered to the rules! The rocker and I never kissed, but we really dug hanging out!

We did regular high school things. He played football, and I was involved in various school activities. When I was in eighth grade, I tried out for the high school dance squad. I was the most, and still am, uncoordinated girl trying out. Needless to say, I did not make the team. This was my first public loss. Val's sister was involved in the flag corps, so instead of dance, I became a flag girl. It was a lot of fun, and we were able to perform with the band when they played at the football games.

At the end of my freshman year of high school, I decided to try out for cheerleader. My mom was a cheerleader in high school, and she encouraged me to try out because of the impact it had on her life. So, still being very uncoordinated, I tried out.

The coaches decided that the junior varsity did not have leadership to guide that squad. So through adult machinations, Val's sister, who should have been on varsity, was held back to give some maturity to the junior varsity squad, and I was placed on varsity. I had a lot of fun that year and made some lifelong friends. However, in the spring, it was tryout time again. My uncoordinated ways got the best of me again, and after a year of varsity, I made JV at tryouts.

The coaches called me the night of tryouts to let me know. I was standing in the kitchen, phone in hand, with my mom, and they said, "Toki, congratulations, you've made junior varsity."

Standing there, stunned and in shock because I did not have a real grasp on how uncoordinated I was, I said, "Thank you, but I will not be filling the slot." I put the phone on the cradle, turned to my mom, and told her the news.

My parents always put the needs of their kids first, and so my mom presented a strong front for me to follow. "That's OK, baby, you will do something else." She hugged me and let me cry.

At the end of my sophomore year in high school, I learned a life lesson: if you want something in life, you have to put your whole heart and soul into obtaining your goal. The experience, though hard at the time, helped mold me into the woman I have become.

My cousin Mud, my soul sister, was a trainer for the football team, and she asked me to join her. This is how I met my high school boyfriend. Mud and this kid were really good friends, and she had a crush on him. She told me she had a thing for him, so what did I do? I became his girlfriend. From the cheerleading experience spawned many events that did, or should have, helped me decide how to make decisions. I should have learned how to be a better person.

The guy Mud had a crush on and I dated for years, but when I look back on how this experience started, what an amazingly jerk thing to do. My cousin had a huge crush on this guy, and I started dating him. Yet another of the bad choices I made in my life.

At eighteen, I moved to Las Cruces, New Mexico, to attend college at NMSU, New Mexico State University. I changed my major almost every year, ranging from journalism to hospitality and tourism. Before I began my fourth year, which was my senior year, I looked at all the credits I had, and because I loved reading, I had the most credits in English, so I decided to graduate with a degree in English. Great, right? The question became, what will you do with a degree in English? A bachelor's in English wasn't opening many doors at the time, but maybe I could be a teacher. I decided the smart thing to do was pursue a master's in education. Getting a bachelor's in English took me four years. So all the friends I had during undergrad were graduating with their bachelor's when I was graduating with my master's.

Because of my Catholic beliefs, I did not have sex until my senior year in college, and it was not with my high school boyfriend, who had become my college boyfriend. I figured at that time, being a senior in college, if something happened and I got pregnant, I could at least get a job to support the child.

6

Do not deprive each other except perhaps by
mutual consent and for a time, so that you
may devote yourselves to prayer. Then come
together again so that Satan will not tempt
you because of your lack of self-control.

—1 Corinthians 7:5

As I was raised Catholic, I was taught not to
fool around with certain things. I was told to always
stay away from tarot cards, horoscopes, fortune-tell-
ing, and Ouija boards. At NMSU, the girls and I
decided it would be fun to play with a Ouija board.

We went swimming at a friend's apartment,
and someone said, "We should play the Ouija board
tonight." We all agreed to meet later that night.

We started playing, and the moment we put our
fingers over the "eye," I felt a vibration in my fingers.
I cannot recall who was there that night except my
friends Christine and Trina. We started asking ques-
tions like, "Will I get married?" and "How many kids
will I have?" But we each had to ask separately so the
"game" would know who was asking.

It said that I would not have a marriage that lasts because my soulmate was still a spirit. When I look back now, I think, *Catholics do not believe in reincarnation.* But at that time, I was buying into it 100 percent.

On our third day of playing, we asked the game, "Who are we speaking to right now?" The game spelled, "Satan." We grabbed the board and threw it and the eye across the room. But we were sucked in and thought it would be OK to continue playing if we moved to a different room. So we went to another room, set the game up, and asked again, "Who are we speaking to?" Again it said, "Satan." So we got up, left the board, and went to a twenty-four-hour restaurant to try to deal with our fear. We couldn't shake it.

The next day, I called our family friend, Fr. Jerry. I told him the whole story about the Ouija board. He said, "Tok, you have to burn the board, and you have to get holy water from the Neumann Center and sprinkle it everywhere you played that game."

So we took the board to an abandoned area and sprayed lighter fluid on it. We threw a match on it and stood and watched it burn. As we watched, a spark flew out and landed on my leg. To this day, on my right thigh, I have a scar that looks like an eye.

A couple of months later, we had a party. I got really drunk and decided I needed to take a shower because that's what I used to do when I got drunk. I passed out in the shower. However, the plumbing was not the best in the house we rented. Some girls came in to check on me. They could not wake me up. They sat me up and tried again. I did finally wake up, and I told them, "God and the devil were fighting over my soul." This event was a spiritually defining point in my life. I opened myself to the evil one, and he was trying to triumph over God in the struggle over me.

In 1995, my brothers, Lou and John, lived in California, and I had been offered a job at a school in Pico Rivera, California. I had a friend who was going to teach English in Korea. He told me I should consider doing it too. I decided to go to Korea to teach English. I was given a job in Seoul, at a Hagwon, a Korean school focusing on language.

When I arrived, the owners of the Hagwon decided it was best if I lived with a Korean family. It was a man and a woman who lived in a two-bedroom apartment. They were nice people, but living in an apartment left little unheard. The neighbor would beat his wife nightly. I hated hearing this because of my experiences with Anne.

In Korea, I also had some private tutoring jobs on the side. One student was an early teenage boy. We would talk and read together. We talked about the beatings I heard, and he told me when he was little, his dad used to hit his mom. She told him, "If you ever have a bruise, rub an egg over it, and it will help get rid of the bruise." If this is true, I cannot say.

The final straw for me was when my co-pre-school teacher called me at the apartment. She asked me to come to the school immediately because she was beaten by her husband. I got there as quickly as I could. When I walked into the room, her face was covered in blood, and her eyes showed bruises.

I asked her, "What did Mr. Kim say?"

She said, "He told me to come into the room and stay here until he came for me."

I stormed out of the room and went to Mr. Kim's door and stood there. He said, "Come in, come in."

"Mr. Kim, how will we help Shelly?"

"Toki, Korea is not the same as America. There is nothing to be done."

"So what you're telling me is that if a man chooses to beat up his wife, that's his prerogative?"

"Well…yes. There is nothing to be done."

"Let me take the classes today, and let her stay here and try to compose herself."

"OK, Toki."

That afternoon, as I was walking to get food, I began to pray. "Lord Jesus, I hate what is happening here. Please be with me. Please don't let me be on this journey alone."

I heard a bird flying behind me, and I turned to look. There was a white dove, which did not fly away. I turned and started walking again, and the little bird landed and started hopping right by me for a few steps to show me I was not alone. Then it was in the air, spreading its beautiful white wings. That moment symbolizes my life.

My mom and Judy, a cousin my mom had grown up with, came to visit me in Korea. Judy's husband, Gary, had worked in Japan, and their family lived there for several years. While I had only been in Korea for six months, the beatings I observed never stopped. My irritation had reached a breaking point when my mom arrived. While they were there, I decided it was time for me to leave Korea, and I got a flight back to the US with them.

The superintendent in Pico Rivera, who had offered me a job, had an open position the following fall. When I came back to Gallup in October, I found an apartment and taught the gifted program at two elementary schools in Gallup.

I then moved to California and taught high school English for two years. My best friends from college, Trina and Christine, moved to California too! We rented a place in Belmont Shores, California.

7

What man of you, having a hundred sheep,
if he has lost one of them, does not leave
the ninety-nine in the open country, and go
after the one that is lost, until he finds it?

—Luke 15:1–7

Teaching in Pico pounded something hard and fast into my thoughts. My students were about 99 percent Hispanic. The teachers were not.

I asked my freshman class one day, "How many of you have been to the beach?" Expecting that because we were thirty minutes from the nearest beach, everyone would raise their hand. My question hung in the air. Not one student, in a class of twenty-four-plus, raised their hand.

Over the week, I surveyed all my classes. Out of five periods of twenty-five-plus students, I had maybe three kids who raised their hands. I was in utter shock. How could this be so in Southern California?

Throughout my first year, I observed how the students were treated. It felt to me as though they were treated like "less-than" students. My dad had eight brothers and sisters. Needless to say, he was a "less-than" student as well. He fell in with the wrong crowd and got into a fight with a kid. His public defender was able to work a deal for him: he would avoid jail time if he left the state of California until he was twenty-one.

So that is why, when I was teaching in California, I saw the students who had never visited a beach and who were treated as "less-than," and I knew I had to go to law school so I could effect change for the "less-than" people.

I started law school in 1999. I met two young men who greatly affected my life, Ray and Cory. Ray, my first husband, is from Franklin Square, New York, and Cory, my second husband, is from Virginia.

I took the California bar and passed, but I did not get a legal job immediately. Instead, I went to work for my law school as a recruiter. Ray and I married in February 2003, after we had graduated from law school. Then Ray received a promotion in his company. He had asked me to marry him before the promotion, and I had said yes immediately. The promotion came with a transfer to St. Louis, Missouri. So off we went, and I sat for the Missouri bar in July 2003 and passed. We decided to move back to California. Ray was doing very well in his company, so they had no problem with the move.

California was where I became a public defender, and I loved my job. First, I did arraignments, then I was moved to domestic violence. When I think back on this now, I wonder how it is that I left Korea because of the domestic violence I observed, but I accepted a position where I defended the accused abusers.

My supervising attorney told me of a legal conference that took place every summer and said he had once attended. He said I should consider going. I went to the conference in the summer of 2007, and I was still married to Ray. At the camp, I met a guy named Steve, and he and I became more than friends almost immediately. We were both married. Ray and I had started a rough patch before I left; he was communicating with other women on the Internet. Needless to say, I was a little peeved.

I called him from the conference and asked, "What percentage do you give us for making it through this?" I was literally asking about his thoughts on our marriage making it. He said, "About a 60–40 chance of us not making it."

After this conversation, it was pretty clear to me that I had no reason to hold back from pursuing the endeavor with Steve, so I did.

Steve is a nice guy who was also a public defender at the time, so we hit it off almost immediately. He always had a little scowl on his face, so I called him Angry Spice. The problem with our situation was that we were both married, and he had a son. I guess because we were removed from everything, we felt as though it was okay to behave this way. Many other people at the camp did not think it was okay and let us know almost immediately. We were not affected and continued our tryst.

When I flew back to California, Ray picked me up at the airport, and I told him we had to go for a hike. On this hike, I told him that we needed to divorce because I had an affair and I knew it was not right for him. During my marriage to Ray, he had let me know that he did not feel comfortable with my friendship with Mr. Cory. So I had backed off from that friendship. When I told Ray that we needed to divorce, nothing was hindering me, so I contacted Mr. Cory again. He was still married to the same woman as he was in law school, and he now had a son.

After my affair with Steve, Ray and I had stopped being "husband and wife." But even in my affair with Steve, I did not use protection because I knew I could not get pregnant. In my first marriage, Ray and I tried to have kids. I couldn't. We went to a fertility specialist, and he told me I would not get pregnant because I didn't have any viable eggs. I wasn't devastated because I thought and said to everyone, "It's OK, I don't need to have kids because I love my work." I felt that in order to have kids, you had to give up what you do as a profession. I was wrong. Maybe I should have asked myself, *Why don't you want kids?* But I didn't.

When I say, "My foot is slipping," your
kindness oh Lord sustains me.

—Psalm 94:18

We were older people. We were all in our thir-
ties, not teenagers who are common to make these
types of decisions. On top of that, we were attorneys.
We were used to being put in situations where spur-
of-the-moment decisions were required. We were
together in a state far off the beaten path because
we were trying to hone our trial skills. The seminar
lasted two weeks.

We decided we would go out drinking that
night. I was the type of person who never did things
in a half-hearted manner, so I drank *a lot*!

"OK, guys, how about we do a shot to com-
memorate our time together," I said this when we
first got to the bar.

"I don't know, Toki, we have to go back tonight,
and we need to make sure someone can drive."

"I hear you, but it will be hours before we leave.
So let's pick a driver, and they can only have one shot.

I'll buy all of our shots!" So we drank a lot—not just drinks, but shots.

It was late, and they started shutting the bar down. I followed Victoria out to our car, which was an SUV that Meriam had rented, so we were all able to pile in. There were five of us in that car. Michelle sat right next to me.

I turned and asked Michelle, "Want to do something crazy?"

I know I chose Michelle because the year before, we had gone white river rafting, and before we got on the raft, we hid behind the tire of a truck and each downed a beer. We hid from everyone because drinking was not supposed to happen at the conference.

"Michelle, what if we try car surfing? But let's not get on the hood, let's do it on the roof!"

We had all been drinking, so it was much easier to persuade Victoria to pull over. I told her I had to pee. I've been told that we were going down the road at a slow speed, about twenty-five miles per hour, as we stood on the roof. We hit a bump in the road. I started to slip off. I grabbed Michelle and pulled her off the car with me. I tried to grab for the rear windshield wiper, and it came off in my hand.

My body smashed down like an accordion. They immediately stopped and got out of the car. What they saw was a big pool of blood around my head. Michelle was conscious and in a lot of pain. We were basically in the middle of nowhere, so there was hardly a cell signal. At the college, we had to walk up a hill to get any reception. Everyone took out their cell phones and tried 911, but no one could get through.

"Maybe we shouldn't move them until an ambulance gets here."

"Are you kidding? We don't even know if we will get an ambulance, and we have to get them to a hospital!"

What I have to keep telling myself is, *We are at an attorney conference!* So everyone involved in this accident was an attorney, and most were civil attorneys. So they all knew that this incident, however it went down, could greatly impact their lives.

They looked down at me and could hear a "death rattle." This is when a gurgling sound comes from someone who has something causing problems with breathing, and usually a death rattle indicates that someone is near death. Sean was a kind man, and he swooped me up in his arms and said, "Zach, get the door."

He got in, and Victoria started to drive to find a cell signal. She thought somewhere near town would be better. As I lay on Sean's lap, I was not fully conscious. They could hear the death rattle, and Zach kept his eyes on me. I kept attempting to do the sign of the cross. I don't know what this looked like, but Zach knew I was a Catholic and knew what the sign of the cross meant to me. When I think on this, I am humbled by my actions. I could barely move, and I was near death, but I was trying to communicate with the Holy Trinity through the sign of the cross.

9

Believe in the Lord Jesus, and you will
be saved, you and your household.

—Acts 16:31

I've been told that when you are in an accident
and recovering from a traumatic brain injury (TBI),
you remember the things you hold fondest. I remem-
ber waking up in the hospital room, looking around,
and thinking, *I must be on a train to California*, like
when we were little and Nana and Pa would take us
to Disneyland. My first thought was, *What will I
have for breakfast? I wonder if Nana will let me have
pancakes.*

Apparently, I had tried to get out of bed several
times. I was rather rough with myself, even pulling
the tracheotomy out of my neck. So they put a tent
around the bed to keep me in. I wasn't on a train; I
was in a hospital room after being in a coma for three
months.

I remember "waking up" in the hospital, and
my mom, dad, and Mr. Cory were there with me.
When I was first in the accident, they called my par-

35

ents from the hospital. They said, "You need to come because we don't think your daughter has much time left." My mom and dad called my brothers, Cory and Ray, and told them what had happened. Christine, Anne, Ray, Mr. Cory, and my brothers traveled to the hospital, several states away. They had put a bolt in my head to monitor the pressure.

They all were standing around my bed in a circle, and my dad said, "Let's pray the 'Our Father.'" They all grabbed hands and prayed over me together.

I was initially hospitalized in Idaho, but I had been flown back to California to recover. Mr. Cory had rented a condo for my parents so that they could stay close to me. I do remember a couple of times, my dad stayed in the hospital room with me, and he told me, "You know, babe, before your accident, I only prayed to Jesus, but after your accident, I started praying to God."

10

Let love and faithfulness never leave you;
bind them around your neck,
write them on the tablet of your heart.

—Proverbs 3:3

By August of 2008, Mr. Cory and I were determined to be together. I had sat for the Illinois bar that July and was talking with everyone I knew who knew attorneys in Illinois to see if I could find a job. The last memory I recall prior to the accident was a call from a friend's attorney boyfriend in Chicago. As there was no cell service at the camp, I was glad he caught up with me before I left.

After the accident, I could not remember many things because my short-term memory had been greatly affected. But my long-term memory was still intact. My dad told me that when I was coming out of the coma, he asked, "Do you know who I am?"

I replied, "Yes, Belantis." To this day, I do not know who Belantis is, but I knew at the time, I loved this man.

As I was in the hospital recovering, I had many visitors, from fellow attorneys from the camp to fellow public defenders. Trina came to visit me; this I do not remember. I am told they asked, "Do you know who this is?" and I could not remember. Of course, my family was there.

My brother Lou helped me learn to walk again, and he followed the doctor's instructions. I had a leash attached to me so that I could not run off, but I could not really walk, much less run! He would spend many hours each day walking me around the hospital. I do not have any recollection of this either. My first memory is of Halloween and the nurses giving me a kitten headband to wear for Halloween.

The condo Mr. Cory rented for my parents was a two-bedroom in Long Beach, California. So my mom, dad, Nana, and Lou were able to stay with me. I was released into their care, and I was to attend occupational therapy daily. My dad would wake up every morning, make coffee for us, and then drive me to therapy. Now this was an event for all, as he obtained his driver's license in New Mexico and was not used to the traffic and puzzle of streets of Los Angeles.

Mr. Cory came to visit every weekend he could get away from his corporate job. The condo was across the street from a strip mall, which was near the Queen Mary. Mr. Cory and I went to a bookstore, and we were looking at the books. We were talking, and he made a comment about his first wife. I got upset, stormed out of the store, and he followed me.

We talked it out, and then he turned to me and said, "Toki, will you marry me?" Of course, I said yes! So even though I had been in an accident and looked different, as my left eye was closed and would not open, he still wanted to be with me.

I was released from OT between Christmas and New Year's. My family, Ray, and Mr. Cory packed up all my things from Ray and my condo, and we drove back to New Mexico. Mr. Cory talked to my parents and me about me moving to Elgin, Illinois, to live with him. All agreed it would be a good idea, as that was the direction we were headed before the accident.

While in law school, Mr. Cory became aware of my close relationship with the Lord and my attendance at Mass every Sunday. As he was raised a Christian, he was dumbfounded that the Catholic church did not allow individuals who had not received the sacrament to receive the Eucharist, and many passionate discussions were had over the years regarding this subject. However, after my accident, and prior to my moving to Illinois, Mr. Cory enrolled in the Rite of Christian Initiation of Adults (RCIA) classes at a parish in Schaumburg, Illinois, in order to become a Catholic. I was going through a very challenging situation, and he knew this would help bring me peace.

As I was raised in a very close-knit family and am extremely close to my brothers, I knew two things in my heart. One, I wanted to marry Mr. Cory, and two, I wanted to have children with Mr. Cory. Being that Mr. Cory already had a son, I knew he would make an excellent sibling! Of course, everyone was aware that I was told I could not have children, but I thought, *Through God, all things are possible, and I should not be alive, but I am.*

11

When a woman is in labor, she is in
anguish because her hour has arrived;
but when she has given birth to a child,
she no longer remembers the pain
because of her joy that a child has
been born into the world.

—John 16:21

Cory and I were on our honeymoon in Bermuda,
and I met a woman at lunch. She asked me a lot of
questions, and I told her that the fertility doctor had
told me I didn't have any eggs and we should con-
sider getting a surrogate. She told me that she had
the "sight." She looked at me and asked, "You're not
pregnant right now?"

I looked at her and said, "No." I thought she
was asking because I had gained a lot of weight since
the accident, and I thought I was chubby and must
look pregnant. However, the woman was correct. I
was pregnant!

In March of 2010, my mom came to Illinois to
visit because we knew the baby would come soon. I

was determined to give birth on March 12, which was the day Pa had passed away in 2003, to honor him. My mom and I went to the store and bought some castor oil. I took two tablespoons because that's what we were told would help the labor along.

On a Friday during Lent, the day started off with the castor oil and went along with nothing eventful happening besides the everyday experience of morning sickness. But about 7:00 p.m., I started to have the "bloody show." The doctors had warned me that this was a sign that the baby was coming, but I couldn't believe it. My mom was there, so she called Mr. Cory.

"Cory, Toki is bleeding. I think she's starting labor."

"OK, Miss Shorty, I'm just across the street. Keep me posted."

The "bloody show" continued, and I started to have a little pain. My mom said, "We gotta get you to the hospital." She called Mr. Cory back and told him I needed to go to the hospital because she thought I had started labor. The hospital was about five miles away, just up the street, so we were there pretty quickly. Cory ran in and told them he thought his wife was in labor.

Up in the room, it seemed like things went very quickly. My ob-gyn came in, looked at me, and said, "OK, Toki, we gotta start pushing." I had gone to the birthing classes, and I had learned all about breathing and the correct way to push. But that didn't seem to be doing the job.

My mom was in the birthing room with Mr. Cory and me, and she was a little nervous, to say the very least. The doctor got a very concerned look on his face and said, "Their blood pressure is dropping. This is dangerous. Toki, we need to get your baby out now."

Then my mom's face got really scared. I think she was having flashbacks of my birth. So I pushed with everything I had in me, and at 11:54 p.m., Cory Louis Watkins was born. He was given Pa's name for his middle name as an homage to him, and I had insisted on naming him Cory, as Mr. Cory was by my side through the accident, recovery, and helped me find a path to normalcy.

My mom and Cory were very concerned about my mental ability to care for my son, so the first day we brought Cory home, Margarita, our nanny, was there to help. I thank God every day that Margarita was there.

Cory was an executive at the business where he worked, so his rule was, "You get up during the night with the baby, because I have to go to work and you don't." Sounds reasonable and logical, but to someone still recovering from TBI and trying to heal her brain, the sleep situation was a mess. Thank God Margarita showed up in the morning.

When I looked at Cory's little face, I knew that we had to give him a playmate. I went back to my ob-gyn. He said, "Toki, as you know, you don't have any more eggs, and it appears that you are in early menopause." I was thirty-eight years old, and I knew I was older, but it seemed unfair to baby Cory.

12

Believe in the Lord Jesus, and you will
be saved, you and your household.

—Acts 16:31

Although we had a lot of sex before getting married, we had not so much after. I was and am a changed person from the one I was before the accident. When I was coming out of the coma, the doctors told Cory that he would have to be a coach to me. That responsibility is a lot to put on someone, and it is too much to ask a person to deal with on a daily basis when you are trying to run a corporation and raise a toddler. So the second time we had sex in our marriage was before I flew back to visit my parents in New Mexico. I threw up on the plane and when I got to my parents' house.

I thought I had the flu. My high school friend was a doctor in town, so I made an appointment. He asked me, "Toki, could you be pregnant?"

I laughed and told him, "I'm in menopause, and I don't have any eggs. I doubt it."

We both laughed, and he said he thought I just had a twenty-four-hour bug. But he planted a bug in my head, so I went and bought a pregnancy test. I took it when I got back to the house. Lo and behold, it came back positive!

I called Mr. Cory, but he was on an international business trip, so I left him a message with the details. A couple of hours later, he called my parents' home phone and left the message, "Hello, Sandovals, this is Joseph. I'm looking for Mary."

As my mom was there when Cory was born, my dad was in Illinois when Walter was born. We went out to eat on June 24, 2011, after I had seen the ob-gyn who told me, "You're due on the fourth, but your baby is not going to wait that long."

At dinner, I told Mr. Cory I thought I was starting labor. He took me to the hospital, and during "hard labor," I was taking a nap.

The nurse said, "OK, Toki, I think your little guy wants to come out," and woke me up. So Walter Griffin Watkins came into the world! Initially, I had wanted to name him Frank after my dad; however, Mr. Cory's father had passed away before he started law school, and while we were in law school, I came to understand how important Mr. Watkins was to Mr. Cory. As my dad and I discussed the baby's name, it became clear that our son's name should be Walter. And when I went to Mass while I was pregnant, each time I took the Eucharist, my child would do flips in my tummy. We were both happy to receive the Lord!

When I look at my life now, what would I be without these two boys? First, I would never know the joy that only the true love for your babies can give you. Second, but for the accident, I would never have stopped the whirlwind of my life to have this experience.

13

For where two or three are gathered together in my name, there am I in the midst of them. For where two or three are gathered in my name, there am I among them. For where two or three gather together as my followers, I am there among them.
—Matthew 18:20

After moving to paradise, St. Thomas, USVI, I started attending CrossFit, and I met an amazing Christian woman, Rachel. Over the years, we became friends, and she invited me to the Bible study she was hosting with her husband. I came to love reading the Bible daily. Through the Bible studies she invited me to join, I have come to a new understanding of asking for prayers. When I had the accident, so many people were asked to pray for me, and so many people did pray for me. I knew this was true, but not the true understanding of "where two or three are gathered."

During Lent of 2018, I went to a confession service. As I sat and talked with God before going to the priest for confession, a thought came to me; this is how He usually communicates with me. I thought, *I did not have an accident, I received a blessing.*

The priest listened to my confession, and for penance, he asked me to read Psalm 32. This was the first time in my life that a priest had really listened to my sins and gave me a penance to reflect upon.

"Blessed is he whose transgressions are forgiven, whose sins are covered. Blessed is the man whose sin the LORD does not count against him and in whose spirit is no deceit. When I kept silent, my bones wasted away through my groaning all day long" (Psalm 32:1–3).

In 2024, my sister-in-law was diagnosed with cancer. Each week at the Bible study, we were asked if anyone needed prayers. I asked for prayers for Rita, and we offered her up to the Lord. Over the next few months, Rita went through radiation and surgery, and we continued to pray. Through the power of prayer and the gentle workings of the Holy Trinity, Rita is now 99.9 percent cancer-free.

This was an "Aha" moment for me. The ladies, through communal prayer, immensely helped Rita. There is definitely strength in the power of two or three praying!

14

Do not fear, for I have redeemed you; I have called you by name, you are mine. When you pass through the waters, I will be with you; and through the rivers, they shall not overwhelm you; when you walk through fire you shall not be burned, and the flame shall not consume you. For I am the Lord your God, the Holy One of Israel, your Savior.

—Isaiah 43:1–3

In 2012, Cory and I divorced. I didn't own a home and have never owned a home, so I found a rental house near him to be close to the boys. My dad, Frank Sandoval, passed away in 2014, and Nana passed away in 2015. In my fifty-two years of life, I have been married and divorced twice. In both cases, I know there is no blame to throw at my ex-husbands.

Ray and I had reached a point in our marriage where we were great friends but had both moved away from being married to each other. In the summer of 2007, when I had my affair with Steve, Ray had gone to New York to visit his family, and he, too, had an affair. We decided to end the marriage, but we had made plans with Christine and AC to go to Cabo San Lucas, so we still went on our trip. All of us had a great time as friends.

Mr. Cory and I started our relationship and fell in love in the fall of 2007. He knew me very well before the accident. When the accident happened, he was there for both my family and me. So much so, the doctors told him, "You are going to have to be her coach because she is going to need someone to push her." The truth is, Mr. Cory did step up, and he did push me, but the role was difficult for both of us. A person who is in love with someone who is in a very serious accident and gets TBI soon realizes that the person is not the same as before. I was changed, and I was struggling to become a functioning person again. So Mr. Cory and I decided to end our marriage as well. However, it was important for us that Cory and Walter see us as amicable and not see two fighting parents.

I am still good friends with both Ray and Mr. Cory. Ray remarried a wonderful woman and now lives in my hometown of Gallup, New Mexico. He has two beautiful children and has become Catholic!

In 2015, Mr. Cory moved the company he worked with to St. Thomas, USVI. When he picked me up from the train station after I had gone to Gallup for Nana's funeral, he told me about the relocation. He said, "I can send the boys to you every summer."

I looked at him completely baffled and said, "I'm on private permanent disability, so I will get paid whether I'm in Gallup, Tijuana, or Taiwan. I just want to be near the boys, so I will move to the Virgin Islands as well."

So in July of 2015, we all relocated to the USVI. It worked out well, as we were both able to have the boys for part of each week. While on the island, Mr. Cory purchased a CrossFit box.

In 2022, I moved back to Gallup to help my mom and make sure she was okay. I planned to come back in May of 2023 because I was asked by Mud's daughter to confirm her. I started looking for a place but could not find anything. I had always planned to go back to the island in May to be with the boys because Mr. Cory had a business trip. I figured while he was away, I could find someplace to live. As the time approached, I still had nothing lined up, and I started to panic. But my auntie Alice told me, "Give it to God." So I did. I placed it at the feet of our Lord and refused to give in to the panic.

Mr. Cory's renter moved out the week before I came back to St. Thomas, so the efficiency apartment Mr. Cory has in his home was available to rent. I see the boys daily now. Mr. Cory travels for work often, so the situation has worked out well for both of us! The other day, my Cory said, "Dad is one of your best friends," and the truth is, without Mr. Cory, my life story would be very different. God is good! The Lord only knows why I was able to conceive with Mr. Cory, but as I have told him, "You gave me the best gifts of my life." When I look at my beautiful boys now, I know I am looking at two living miracles. Cory and Walter are my presents from God. I'm not lucky; I'm blessed. God is good!

About the Author

Toki Sandoval is a cradle Catholic, and the Holy Trinity has walked with her since birth. She has a bachelor's degree in English, a master's in Curriculum and Instruction, and a juris doctorate. She has lived in New Mexico, California, Missouri, Illinois, and St. Thomas, US Virgin Islands.

She has taught the gifted program at two elementary schools in Gallup, New Mexico, English at a high school in Pico Rivera, California, and she has sat for the bar in California, Missouri, and Illinois. She also practiced law in Missouri as a prosecutor and in California as a public defender.

Fifteen years ago, she was involved in an accident in which she injured herself and incurred Traumatic Brain Injury. Over the past fourteen years, she has been a stay-at-home mom, attempting to succeed at the hardest job she's ever held: motherhood. She thanks the Holy Trinity daily for blessing her with amazing opportunities.

The reader is encouraged to visit her social media pages: Facebook under Toki Sandoval or Instagram under @tokimarie.

www.ingramcontent.com/pod-product-compliance
Lightning Source LLC
Chambersburg PA
CBHW022116150726
47990CB00003B/1374